"There is nothing in machinery, there is nothing in embankments and railways and iron bridges and engineering devices to oblige them to be ugly. Ugliness is the measure of imperfection."
H. G. Wells

INDEX

COPYRIGHT

ISBN-13: 978-1537642062
ISBN-10: 1537642065

Principal publishers:
Timeline Books, Folkestone, England.

DEDICATION

To My
Mum, Dad and Grandparents

United again in Heaven

INTRODUCTION

Have you ever tried to describe a phobia?

It's not very easy at all to outline the morbid or unreasonable fear you have towards something, especially when trying to explain it to family or friends - or even strangers - who refuse to understand what you go through with it day after day.

So, what *is* a phobia?

The Oxford English Dictionary describes it as being "a strong unreasonable fear of something". Yeah, that just about sums up quite succinctly what I have!

Imagine, if you will, going through life having an excruciating hatred towards some inanimate object that you just know deep down should not harm you. Yet, the irrational part of your 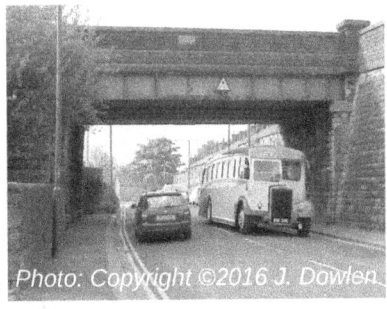 Photo: Copyright ©2016 J. Dowlen brain says, "that's bad; that's so, so bad". In my case it is steel (or iron) constructed railway bridges (also known as plate girder bridges, like seen in the picture here, taken at Skipton, North Yorks).

The nearest descriptive word I can find to relate to my phobia is 'gephyrophobia' but, although that is a fear of bridges, it is more related to *crossing* them, which is not my actual problem. There is another word, called 'batophobia', which is a fear of being close to tall buildings. This, unfortunately, is not too accurate, either, as I don't have a problem with tall buildings. So, the conundrum remains about this; just what long name (if any) is used to describe the inexplicable fear of being near railway bridges? And, the more ornate they are, the worse my reaction is towards them.

Please keep in mind that this is not a book about how to cure a phobia; it is about my own particular (and peculiar) phobia and how I have learned to cope with it. I make no medical or scientific claims and none should be construed, expected or anticipated by readers. I am no expert on phobias and I don't profess to be but, like many people, I strive to try and understand them.

From time to time during the following pages, I will refer to my wife Myra, Grandfather (Grandad), Grandmother (Nan), my Mum and Dad and one or two other relatives. These mentions are for reference purposes only and are not meant to be interpreted that this book is a family history publication.

My story is the nearest I can get to describing my phobia and how it affects me virtually every day of my life. You may find it fascinating, you might not. Either way, I've told it like it is, no exaggerations or gimmicks.

By the very nature of this subject matter, I was not going to make this book a pictorial publication, but I have painfully included some illustrations on the following pages of railway bridges. I thank my friend Jerry Dowlen for taking time out from his busy schedule to snap some of the photographs to include as examples.

Is mine really the world's strangest phobia? Please read on and decide for yourself.

Trevor Mulligan
Railway Bridge Phobic

Why Are Phobias Kept Secret?

There is a semblance of embarrassment about phobias that nobody seems able to understand or explain satisfactorily. As an example, I have kept my strangest of phobias 'below the radar' for most of my life and nobody except my closest family knew about it. Even then, some of them have either laughed it off or wiped the information from their memory. Obviously, now, everyone who reads this book will learn of my heart-stopper, but I no longer feel embarrassed by it.

To maybe prove my point, when I searched on the internet recently for 'why are phobias kept secret?', I couldn't find a single reference to an appropriate answer. I found plenty of links relating to 'how to cure a phobia', but nothing on why people don't openly talk about their own irrational fears of objects that are not known to physically harm them.

One search result that truly made me cringe was an answer given by someone, to a question raised about somebody who was inexplicably afraid of a lotus pod, "You may be suffering from post traumatic stress disorder". Really?!! So, I wonder how that works for the phobic who asked the question, and I wonder even more how, why, when and where such a generalised response would relate to my own phobia?

It seems that, the more you question the very existence of a phobia, the more questions arise to be answered. As an offshoot to my original question about why phobias are kept to themselves by the ever-suffering phobics, I changed my search parameter to 'what causes a phobia to manifest itself?'

I read some information where a statement was made that not all phobias are common. Aha! At least I've belatedly discovered that my own phobia towards railway bridges could actually be uncommon. So, where does that lead me and my Achilles heel?

My research went on to reveal that there's hardly anything that wouldn't cause a phobic reaction to anyone. Phobias tend to have their own group types, too; the fear of animals (domestic or wild), things around us (yes, I'll claim membership of that group, as railway bridges are all around us), anything medical like being jabbed with a needle the size of a jousting lance and so on.

I also discovered that, if you suffer with a phobia so much that you change the way you live your life to avoid it, you need 'specialist help'. Okay, that sounds very much like a prelude to a money-making venture for someone, with no absolute guarantee of a cure at the end of the 'treatment'.

Elsewhere, I found that strong phobias could be inherited. Strange as it may sound, I looked further into this aspect and I couldn't trace anybody in my family who's had to avoid railway bridges all their life. And, further, if I went back in time far enough, this phobia wouldn't have existed before the 1830s, because no railways would have existed anywhere in the world for there to be a need for such bridges. Which leaves the final conclusion that fear is believed to derive from fear itself.

This can probably be best described as a 'Catch-22' situation. You do not wish to suffer from a phobia, so you try to extinguish it by meeting the problem head-on, but when you try it causes anxiety and fear for you once more. This invariably results in the panic getting a strong foothold until you develop a total rejection towards that which irks you. In other words, you become totally obsessed with avoiding the 'problem' altogether - a full-blown phobia.

And so we come full circle back to square one; why do people keep their phobias to themselves?

Maybe that's as far as I am going to get with trying to find out why people keep their phobias under wraps. I could hazard a guess or two (or three, or four...) and suggest that it's shame felt towards being ridiculed by their peers; that would most probably be the nearest real reason for such secrecy.

And, what about the cause of a phobia? Well, in my own case, it could have been due to being exposed to steel railway bridges at a very young age in the late 1950s or early 1960s, when my Grandad took me to Bermondsey to see my Great Aunt Polly. Up until then, the only road-crossing railway supports I had known were the nine arches that make up the viaduct spanning the Cray Valley in St Mary Cray, and the fairly innocuous steel bridge that crosses Cray Avenue, just a short stroll down Station Approach from St Mary Cray railway station.

Although the viaduct itself was widened from south to north in 1958, to accommodate two tracks instead of the original single reversible track, I am not old enough to remember the original viaduct, so I've only ever had memories of how that crossing is today. Being exposed to a viaduct in London that has been widened and strengthened several times since the 1830s most probably levered me right out of my comfort zone and deeply into the 'Twilight Zone'.

Underneath The Arches:
St Mary Cray

Let me take you back to the 1950s, a time of the birth of Rock 'n' Roll, of Bill Haley and His Comets; of the Suez Crisis; of the Matthews F A Cup Final at Wembley.

It is 1958 and work is being carried out on the St Mary Cray railway viaduct, to transform it from a single reversible track running across the top of the arches, serving both northbound and south-bound rail commuters to a two-line crossing.

What's strange about that? Well, nothing, unless you are local to the area and you do or did firmly believe that the current viaduct is how it was built back in the Victorian era.

At first glance (right), there does not appear to be anything particu-larly unusual about the viaduct. The nine arches are still there (even though they are not all showing up in my

photo) and it still spans the High Street. However, there is a big difference to its original erection in the late 1850s, compared to now. The viaduct itself is one hundred percent wider now than when it was originally built.

Back in 1958, roughly around one hundred years since the railway came to the village, the service on the Swanley line was increased in capacity, which meant that there had to be two lines crossing the Cray Valley instead of the original one line. This, in turn, resulted in the need for the St Mary Cray viaduct to be widened to accommodate the extra track. Not a mean feat, by any stretch of the imagination!

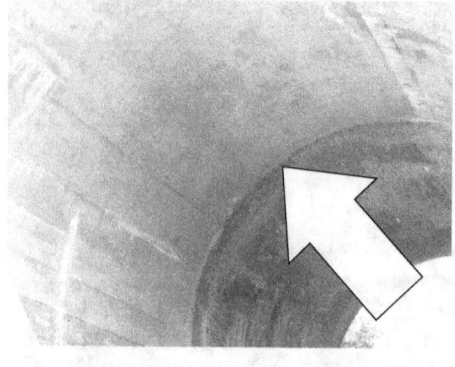

Rather than construct a second viaduct or bridge to run alongside (but separate from) the existing one, the decision was made to extend the width of the crossing, and the end result can be seen on my next photo (left). You can see the join under the arch (indicated by an arrow), which shows where the two separate constructions merge (the newer section being nearer to my camera lens). You could say, quite plausibly, that St Mary Cray has two viaducts and not one.

The original viaduct, on the north (St Paul's Cray) side consists of being all brickwork, but the extension on the south (St Mary Cray) side is a combination of brick spandrels and support work with concrete making up the inner round-headed arches. This can be seen more clearly in this next photo (below), which I took looking straight upwards towards the curvature of the arch.

NEW
(Concrete)

OLD
(Brickwork)

It is difficult nowadays to find a photograph of just the viaduct as it appeared before 1958, but the next two photos (page 20) are the best examples I have managed to source so far.

The first photo below was taken on May Day 1892. The viaduct is clearly viewed in the background, and it can also be seen that the arches are not very wide from south to north, i.e. under the bridge.

Similarly, the second photo below (taken around the turn of the 19th into the 20th century) also strongly indicates that the viaduct has no substantial 'thickness', when compared to the modern-day arches.

From A Young Age

For as long as I can remember, I 've had this hang up about railway bridges. Don't ask me why, because I have never managed to fathom it out; what I do know, however, is that this irrational fear has been (and still is) a right royal pain in the backside for me since early childhood.

I have suffered indubitably since my Grandad took me to visit some of our relatives in Bermondsey when I was about the age of 5 years old. I'd been staying with my grandparents in East Dulwich for about a week or so, give or take, something I was to continue doing once a year during the school summer holidays in the early 1960s. Little outings on the London buses were all part and parcel of that adventure.

All went well at the start; we caught the bus from East Dulwich to somewhere quite a walk away from my Great Aunt Polly's house in Bermondsey. As I was very young, I didn't make a note as to where the bus stopped for us to get off. En route to her house, we had to walk past a play area with swings, roundabout, climbing frame, mechanical horse and so forth. I was allowed to play there for a few minutes, while Grandad rolled some 'Sun Valley' tobacco into a cigarette paper and smoked it.

After we prepared to move away from the playground, it took a while for me to notice them... a whole line of brick arches holding up the many railway lines that took trains into and beyond London Bridge station to the north and New Cross, Greenwich and beyond in the south. To think about them now still makes me shudder and the hairs stand up on the back of my neck, just as they did back then. I have no idea why; to me, they represent fearfulness at its highest. But, my Grandad was there to reassure me that there was nothing to be afraid of, although I thought otherwise.

I was rooted to the spot; I would not let go of the chain that supported the swing I'd just vacated. I felt like doing a piddle, a poo and throw up all at the same time. Fortunately, for all concerned and to spare my Grandad any public embarrassment, I did none of those. In order to get to our destination, we had to walk underneath one of the arches, and I wasn't best keen to do it. So, I gripped onto my Grandad's hand as tightly as I could, held my breath and made a dash for it. Once the other side, I should have been pleased with my achievement, but I wasn't.

But what I met with a short while later had me shouting my lungs out and I could probably have been heard all around South London!

Copyright ©2016 J. Dowlen

I was aware that the road we were walking along ran parallel to the railway lines, about 40 or 50 feet away from us to our right. I had assumed that there would be quite long arches all along the underside of the railway. Rows of houses and maybe commercial premises blocked out our view, so I was relatively calm about walking along, especially having just shortly before negotiated bravely (for me!) walking under the long, low arch nearest to the playground. And then we got to the end of the road, where a T-junction met with Spa Road...

We looked left in the direction of Aunt Polly's house and there was no problem but, when we looked right, oh, my goodness!! My heart sank, bounced somewhere near my young groin and then came right up into my mouth, dislodged only when I let out the loudest "Nooooooo!" screech you could ever imagine.

Copyright ©2016 J. Dowlen

There, as even now I shudder to think about it, was the most horribly scary railway bridge imaginable spanning the road at an angle.

It was very, *very* dark underneath it and I could not see the 'far end' of the road that disappeared into the expanse, maybe due to the angle at which we viewed it, albeit all too briefly by me. The number of different rail lines on top of the bridge must have been so vast, laying side by side, that daylight must have been kept out for at least half a mile (or so it seemed to this young and quivering wreck of a boy). In fact, it was probably only a hundred yards or so, maybe even 200 yards.

Yet again, I was rooted to the spot where I stood, in disbelief, my right hand by now shielding my eyes in denial. My Grandad was beginning to chuckle; I doubt he'd ever come across such an adverse reaction to something that obviously never bothered him or any of the residents living in the area. But, in his own way, he was understanding. To a point. He kept referring to the monstrosity as a 'viaduct'. At that tender young age, I couldn't understand that. What we had spanning our High Street in St Mary Cray... *that* was a viaduct. This thing in Bermondsey was a series of ugly tunnels and steel bridges and it scared seven shades of crap out of me.

We eventually moved on and turned left at the junction into Spa Road, walking away from the bridge, thank goodness, and arrived at my Aunt's front door. I couldn't get into her house quickly enough! Grandad eventually placated me, once inside, but it took a sterling effort on his part to calm me down. I'd been spooked beyond belief. Aunt Polly got around to asking what all the commotion was about, to which my Grandad replied that something about the 'viaduct' had scared me. Too bloody right it did! My Aunt tried to reassure me by mentioning that they live with that railway line, and all the bridges and arches in the local streets, every single day and there's nothing bad with them.

But I was having none of it.Even as young as I was, I knew what I didn't like, and I certainly didn't like that bridge or anything adjoining it. I don't recall how long we stayed at that house, but I was dreading having to run (or walk) the gauntlet of all those arches on the way back to get our bus. Even though I couldn't see most of them, I knew they were there, and that was enough to keep me on edge.

Oh, boy, my Grandad then offered to walk me *under* the offending bridge just to prove there was nothing to fear. But this very unimpressed kid declined this offer very dramatically. All I wanted to do was get back to the bus stop a hundred miles away from that place and return to East Dulwich. At five years old, I had had an early warning that I was to be stuck with one of the strangest, if not unique, phobias known to mankind. And, I would grow to try and avoid the confrontational ability of steel railway bridges whenever and wherever I could.

We made that same trip to Bermondsey twice more after that; my Nan was either at her part-time job, or at one of her day meetings at her local church hall, and my Grandad couldn't leave me with anyone else. I was also too young to be left 'home alone', so I had to endure my torture of running the Bermondsey Viaduct gauntlet on both those occasions. And, of course, with each of those further times I went the apprehension, negative anticipation and anxiety got much worse, as I knew what to expect. That made it much more stomach-churning than the first time, as on that introductory occasion I knew very little about the consequences that were to follow and haunt me until this very day.

I am given to understand that most of the arches along that stretch of the viaduct in Bermondsey now house shops or restaurants or places of that ilk, but the whole area still haunts me so much that I've never been back there to find out for myself.

My mum was born in Spa Road in 1920 and spent the early part of her life growing up there. I guess she, like my Grandad, was used to the 'viaduct'.

Spa Road Station

Spa Road in Bermondsey, South London, has boasted its very own station three times since the earliest days of railway travel in London. Local knowledge has it that, the original incarnation was opened in February 1836 and, by all accounts, it was a crude affair, with low-lying platforms positioned tightly either side atop a two-line viaduct. A somewhat rickety wooden stairway, positioned up the outer side of the viaduct, gave access to the platforms, as can be seen in the image below.

That station, which was the first terminus ever built in Greater London, closed in December 1838 after the track was extended to London Bridge. However, a new station appeared at Spa Road in 1842, following a successful application to Parliament by the London & Greenwich Railway

(L&GR) in 1840 to widen the viaduct, from two lines to four lines, to accommodate the vast increase in rail traffic towards London Bridge from outlying regions in the south-east of England.

The second station was built on the site of the old one, when the South Eastern Railway took over from the L&GR. That station closed in 1867, as a result of it being dismantled and moved 200 yards along the track.

The third and final Spa Road Station, in its new location, opened later in 1867 and closed in 1915 due to a World War One employment 'economy drive'. It was apparently still used as an alighting and boarding point for local railway workers, between 1915 and 1925, after which the station closed down completely.

Some sections of the station remain to this day, along with some signage on the arches below. At the time of its final closure, the viaduct supporting Spa Road Station had increased in width exponentially, supporting eleven tracks towards London Bridge and twelve tracks towards the south.

Spa Road Station was called into action one more time, in 1999, as an evacuation point for passengers following a train derailment. I would not have liked to have been a passenger on that train, having to be evacuated down and into the full clutches of those viaduct arches and bridges below, giving rise to my phobia once more.

Spa Road Station, circa 1908

Two plaques placed on the brick arches in Bermondsey
serve as a reminder of the former Spa Road Station.
Photo: Copyright ©2016 Jerry Dowlen.

Avoiding Places

Most major towns and cities around the world have a rail network running through or into them, and many of those places contain steel bridges which span the road and river thoroughfares with few exceptions. I am only naming just a few examples here, but I am more than understanding of the fact that many more could be added to my inexhaustive list.

All my life I've been saddled with the morbid fear of steel railway bridges. And some types of brick arches as well, but much lesser so. During my younger days, it was purgatory for me if I went out anywhere different with my parents. I would always be hoping that the next corner we walked around wouldn't result in us confronting one type of bridge or another.

Unfortunately, that happened more times than you can imagine, especially when we visited my grandparents in Dulwich. Being a part of the ever-expanding Greater London, most areas of South London have railway lines passing through them overhead at some point or another, a fact of life that I realised during my growing up years when visits to such locations ended in consternation for me.

Quite often, during holiday stays in Dulwich, my Nan would take me shopping in Rye Lane at Peckham. Each time we went, I didn't want to go. Why? Well, the main street of shops not only has a steel railway bridge across it, it has *two* of them! And they both gave me the jitters. If we had to go to Jones & Higgins, to name but one department store back then, we had to walk under both bridges to get to it. And then walk under them again on the way back to the bus stop.

My heart always sank and I felt like I had insects crawling up and down my neck each time we did that. It was a horrible feeling and, having a lemonade while my Nan enjoyed a cup of tea in the Lyons Corner House cafe didn't make things any better, because the entrance to the place was right next to one of the bridges! I couldn't wait to grow up quickly enough so that I didn't have to be put through so much painful torment ever again.

I've been back to Peckham only once in my adult years, to get my car repaired, but that was over 40 years ago now and I don't miss the place or its double distraction one bit. If they take the bridges away from Rye Lane then I'd be only too glad to go back there to do some shopping; but they won't, so I can't.

Talking about more than one bridge in the same place, I still find it less than enthralling each time I pass under the twin railway bridges at Shortlands, near Bromley. I'm always driving my car when I do pass under then, usually taking my wife Myra to King's College Hospital at Camberwell to see the specialist about her illness, but they are no less scary monsters to me. Even more so when the traffic lights at the junction are at red and I have to sit staring, for what seems like a very uncomfortable lifetime, at my steely nemeses.

Yes, highly irrational, you may say. On the verge of jocular, possibly. But, to me, this phobia I have is very real and is no laughing matter.

Another place I dread to visit is New York in America. It doesn't take a rocket scientist to realise that New York has an elevated railway, and it is supported by a continuous steel-girdered raised bridge system. I know that, without ever having been there but from watching car chases in films and TV shows, I would freeze on sight if I was walking down a street and turned at the next junction to be faced with that! A typical example of what I mean can be seen in the film 'The French Connection', wherein Popeye Doyle, a police detective played by actor Gene Hackman, was involved in a now-iconic car chase under the elevated railway tracks in Brooklyn, as he followed a hijacked train travelling at speed on the track above him. To me, the construction doesn't bear thinking about, yet it dictates my life enough for me not to want to even experience the... er... experience.

Since sitting down to prepare my manuscript for this book, I have found out that Chicago also maintains an elevated railway system, in a simi-  lar vein to that of New York (see photo). So, Chicago is yet another place I am now prepared to strike off my list of places to visit. This elevated railway can be evidenced in the film called 'While You Were Asleep', in which actress Sandra Bullock plays a ticket office clerk at a station on that same railway system.

I cannot deal with the potential panic that these places would present to me and my phobia, so I'd rather not visit them to find out. I do not have, nor ever have had, masochistic tendencies and I don't intend to start having them now.

Conversely, up until the 1950s, Liverpool on Merseyside had its own overhead railway network which would have certainly stopped me from visiting the place. The Liverpool Overhead

Railway system closed down in 1956, and was demolished in 1957, but the steel structure would have unnerved me for sure had I ever physically seen it in place.

I remember a trip that I made to Boulogne over in France with some of my work friends back in 1988.The ferry port at Folkestone wasn't far from where I lived at the time, so it was quite a regular outing for us. The old town of Boulogne, if you have never been there, is a fortified place surrounded by ramparts (believed to be from Roman times) and entry is via a number of arched stone gateways. The old town has many avenues and streets to explore, so much so that subsequent visits need to be arranged as not all the places can be visited in one trip. Anyway, back to the point; my friends and I chose to walk up a street we'd never been along before... and, about halfway along, I stopped and froze in my tracks. There ahead, about 500 yards away, was a steel monster spanning the road. My friends asked me what was wrong, as they later mentioned I had turned very white, so I tried to explain to them about my phobia. In fact, while I told them of my aversion, I had to turn away from the direction of the bridge to face the other way, towards the town centre.

Similarly, back in Bermondsey again, there's a hideous monster that stretches across Southwark

Park Road that I will not under any circumstances go anywhere near, let alone spite my phobia by trying to walk under it! Even as a passenger on a bus, or maybe even driving in my car, if I get anywhere near visual distance of that bridge it gives me the willies.

A place I used to frequent in my teen years was Crystal Palace Football Club's ground at Selhurst Park in South London. The Palace have been my football club of choice since my schooldays, and a bunch of us used to catch the mid-morning train from Orpington Station, change first at Beckenham Junction and again at Crystal Palace to get the branch line round to Selhurst Station.

 After walking down the slope from the platform to the street, we'd turn left towards the football ground, which was about a quarter of a mile away. If I looked backwards over my shoulder, there was a set of two steel bridges spanning the road, to the right of the slope we'd walked down. Fortunately, we didn't have to walk under them, going to or returning from Selhurst Park, but they were there all the same (above left)...

Further afield, and on the other side of the world, the Sydney Harbour Bridge in Australia represents a humungous and frightening landmark for me and my phobia. Although it carries just two tracks over and above the waterway, it is the sheer size and construction material it is made out of that has always prevented me from walking into the travel agents and booking a flight to 'Down Under'. Sorry, Australia, the rest of your country may not be as daunting as Sydney but the way this infliction affects me I can't take any chances. Not in this life-time, anyway.

Now here's the strangest of things, and something which may eliminate steel as being a root cause of my phobia. I took Myra to Paris for a weekend break back in the 1990s. This was before there was any sign of, and she was diagnosed with, the chronic illness that has since disabled her. Anyway, we did what all visitors to Paris do, we went to see the Eiffel Tower. The Tower is constructed of steel cross-members and I was pleasantly surprised that I had no adverse reaction to this. No phobia problems whatsoever except, of course, the more generalised lack of enthusiasm for going up to the top!

Back in the 1970s, when the main line train drivers of what was then the government-owned British Rail were on strike, I had to try and find alternative ways to get back home to Orpington each evening after work in the City of London. One way I followed was to catch the tube from Tower Hill to East Ham, ride on the 101 bus to the Woolwich Ferry and walk through the looooong pedestrian tunnel beneath the River Thames. Once on the south side, I caught either the 51 or 229 bus back to Orpington. Yes, it took a few hours longer than usual to get home that way, but my point is actually related to the pedestrian tunnel itself. Anyone reading this account, who suffers from claustrophobia, can quite rightly imagine that the tunnel is fear fodder exemplified to claustro-phobics. The fact that I could walk through that tunnel and not be affected by feeling closed in also confirms that claustrophobia is not a reason for my phobia of railway bridges.

Myra and I have also been to Venice, Italy, and rode in a gondola and also on a couple of river buses while we were there. The canal system in Venice flows under many pedestrianised bridges, and I never had a problem with any of those, either.

When I worked in London, I didn't think twice about walking along the pedestrian underpasses (subways) to get from one side of a busy road to the other side. Likewise, I was always quite happy to use the London Underground rail network when required to do so. And, I never went into a blind panic if I took a stroll along the Thames

Embankment and had to walk underneath the many road bridges, although I did still try to avoid the high railway crossing leading out of Charing Cross Station.

Now, I don't usually scare easily, but railway bridges do spook me every time. You are probably muttering to yourself that there's absolutely no logic to this type of fear and, to an extent, I'll agree with you. But, I must also suggest that you come and live for a month in my skin and then afterwards see if you have the same viewpoint. I don't *want* to have a phobia about railway bridges, but I've got one, and it is very painful to endure when the very things I have a problem with are scattered all around this country and beyond.

RAILWAY BRIDGE FACT

Who is it that we have to blame for the introduction of steel support bridges? No, it isn't Isambard Kingdom Brunel this time. The first iron bridge was designed by Thomas Pritchard and built by Abraham Darby (The Third) to span the River Severne at Telford, Shropshire as far back as 1779 (two years after Pritchard's death). Steel bridges came along much later, in the early part of the 20th century. Every railway line planner after this appears to have thought that the initiative to use steel in bridge construction was a great idea. *I think otherwise!*

However, it is only my own opinion, based on my phobia, that our countryside, towns and cities have been blighted more than enough by these unsightly behemoths.

CHANNEL TUNNEL FACT

When I worked in France prior to my early retirement, it was estimated that I had travelled back and forth through the Tunnel more than five thousand times over a fifteen year period.

I live quite close to the Channel Tunnel, which links Kent (and, by association, the UK) to France and the rest of mainland Europe by a series of rail services, and I think maybe that the Eurostar railway line planners realised, at an early stage in its development, what a folly it would have been to scar the Kent countryside with more of the same old ugly steel bridges, where the Eurostar tracks now cross over the A20 trunk road just outside of Cheriton. Instead, they sensibly opted for concrete-constructed over-passes and, through doing so, have kept this steel bridge phobic very happy! Alas, I doubt somehow that they were thinking about me or my phobia at the time.

Working In London

*"Let me take you by the hand and lead you
through the streets of London..."*
*"Streets of London", by Ralph McTell,
reached number 2 in the UK Pop Chart in 1974*

One of the provisos about me agreeing to work in the City of London was that I did not wish to encounter any railway bridges to walk under. That's a bit of a tall order if you know London well. Certain parts of the City have railway bridges spanning the roads there at every different angle imaginable. Not a bed of roses experience for this lad, it must be said.

Despite assurances from those closest to me, the only ones who knew of my knee-buckling phobia about bridges, that there were no problematic issues for me in that part of Town, I found out to my utter dismay and disappointment that the opposite was true when I arrived at London Bridge station on my very first morning. Having travelled up from Petts Wood during the morning rush hour, I alighted from the train and headed towards the general direction of London Bridge itself. It was quite easy to find; I just followed the crowd of raised umbrellas aloft the suited gents in bowler hats. That's not a cliché, it really was like that, on the very rainy February morning in 1971!

Unfortunately for me, however, the London Bridge of the time (and still currently) was a replacement for the old one that had been sold to someone in America (who, rather unfortuitously for him, thought he was buying Tower Bridge), and the new one was still being constructed.

Pedestrians were diverted via a brick tunnel under the tracks above and round onto the Bridge. That made me have kittens, and at first I was rooted to the spot when I saw where I had to walk, but as there was no other route it was either do it or not go to work. If I'd chosen the latter option, my thirty eight years in the Civil Service might never have got off the ground.

The first few years of my employment consisted of working in an office where the building was a short walk from Fenchurch Street Station. A bit further away, heading towards Whitechapel, is an area known as The Minories. The streets there lay alongside but below the bridges supporting the railway tracks running out of and into Fenchurch Street. Whenever I walked around the area, I glanced at the solid steel-membered railway bridges from a distance but never had the need or desire to get close to or walk under them. The bridge spanning Mansell Street is supported by several columns which makes it look even more scary to me than it needs or ought to be.

At one time, when I used to drive to the office in Mark Lane, I often parked my car near Leman Street in Whitechapel and walk from there into work. Leman Street itself has been made quite famous in recent times by being the feature base of a BBC TV drama series called 'Ripper Street'. Yes, Leman Street does really exist and so does the police station, although the film set in the programme is no doubt situated on location elsewhere.

When I used to walk past Leman Street along Cable Street and into Royal Mint Street, I came perilously close to the double railway bridges that cross the southern tip of Leman Street. I used to shield the side of my face with my hand so that I didn't have to look at them! If there had been other options at the time, I'd have made alternative car parking arrangements for sure, but free parking is free parking which was at a premium in London then and is non-existent now.

It wasn't always possible for me to avoid my arch enemy (please excuse the pun). Back in the early 1980s, I worked in a building on the South Bank of the River Thames, and there were three routes that I could have taken to get to work. One way was to arrive by train at Blackfriars and walk across the road bridge from the north side to the south side of the Thames. Another way was to catch a train to Waterloo East and that had its own moments, as I had to walk past several shops built into the arches underneath the railway and then walk under a steel bridge, which worried me considerably the first few times I had to do it. And the third route was by car along Stamford Street, driving under a big steel bridge at the traffic lights intersection with Blackfriars Bridge Road. Even though I was driving each time, I would shiver immensely when I drove under that bridge, especially if the traffic lights were red and I had to remain stationary under it.

Directly outside Blackfriars Station there used to be a steel bridge that spanned Ludgate Hill and supported the tracks leading to and from the Holborn Viaduct terminus. That bridge has now been removed after the introduction of the Thameslink service, but that wasn't until I had walked under it every working weekday for more than a year.

Railway bridge spanning Ludgate Hill,
Blackfriars, circa 1927

Checking Towns and Cities On Street Maps

Whenever I go anywhere that is new to me, I check out the location on a street map or on the internet. If one or the other shows no signs of the tell-tale black lines, that represent railway tracks, then I'm happy. On the contrary, if there are lines drawn across any of the roads then I start to get very fidgety and uncomfortable.

I remember on one occasion in the late 1970s that I drove one of my brothers up to London for some reason. We landed up somewhere with many ugly lumps of metal across the road above us. It was a real nightmare scenario for me; it didn't seem to matter which road or direction we took, there were steel railway bridges everywhere. I thought I saw a sign saying we were in King's Cross, but that might also have just been a signboard directing traffic there.

More fool me, I guess, for taking a wrong turning somewhere. I think now, looking back some thirty-odd years later, we should have been in the centre of London and instead we'd wandered a bit off course. Wherever I steered my car it seemed we were confronted with these bloody dark and dingy abominations spanning the roads. I was starting to get very restless and uneasy and couldn't wait to find a road sign that would get us away from that spine-shivering place. I had nightmares about that place for several weeks afterwards and even recalling it now fills me with dread.

It was around that time that I decided to take more notice of the homework I needed to do, in relation to how the railway network intermingles with the road system in every town and city from here to Timbuktu, as well as how it interferes with me living as normal a life as possible without being scared witless.

When Myra first became ill, however, we had to attend the neurological unit at Guy's Hospital in London. I didn't know it at the time, but Guy's is situated in St Thomas Street, which runs parallel to Tooley Street just south of the River Thames, but on the southern side of London Bridge Station (which also runs parallel with both roads). That really served me right, because I hadn't done my homework by checking my London street maps book beforehand. In between Guy's Hospital and Tooley Street, there's a very long bricked arch tunnel that runs beneath the many tracks that form the station above. This encompasses a one-way street that links St Thomas Street to Tooley Street; most of the other arches along that stretch are enclosed and contain business premises with ornate frontages, except for the one-way traffic tunnel leading traffic away from St Thomas Street. At first, the whole set up worried me, my phobia pushing my feelings to the extreme. But, the more times we went up to Guy's - which was every couple of months or so at the time - the more I got used to the landscape, although the entanglement of bridges across the road further down towards Tower Bridge Street still couldn't be my friends.

Another challenge for me arose when Myra was taken into King's College Hospital in Camberwell on three separate occasions for treatment and tests for her illness. Instead of worrying about the time factor and difficulty involved in travelling up to London each day from our home on the south Kent coast, I booked into guest houses in the West Dulwich area and caught a bus from there to the hospital. In order to get to the hospital the bus had to pass under railway bridges at both Tulse Hill and Herne Hill railway stations. No big deal, you may say, but it was a very big deal for me and I found that closing my eyes as we went under the bridges helped to a small extent.

But that bridge across the road at Herne Hill and I have previous 'issues'. Back in the early 1970s, I was invited to have a trial for a Sunday football team at Brockwell Park, which is opposite Herne Hill railway station. I arrived in all innocence at

Herne Hill on that Sunday morning and made my way towards the entrance to the park when... wham! I clapped eyes on that fearsome steel railway bridge. Fortunately, I did not have to venture underneath it, but the shock was so intense that it affected my game. Unsurprisingly, I flunked what should have been a relatively easy trial to get into that team.

Railway Bridges
In Media Backdrops

I am not sure if TV and film companies are trying to give me the jitters, but there's an awful lot of films, plays, commercials and documentaries that are using railway bridges and tunnels as backdrops. Perhaps the location managers for each shoot think that the bridges are a much underused part of the landscape.

Here's a big 'for instance' example, although it doesn't relate to London. I won't go to Manchester; not because I don't like it there - how could I know, when I've never been there? - but because it has many railway bridges and brick arches spanning their roads and walkways. If you want proof, just look at 'Coronation Street' on TV. That's got an old railway line now converted to a tramway, running behind the houses and the 'Rovers Return' pub, with an arched bridge across the road almost beside the pub. Okay, so the show is based in fictional 'Wetherfield', on a custom-built outside studio, but they do quite a bit of 'outside the studio lot' filming under railway bridges in nearby Manchester. If you've never noticed, have a look next time one or more of the cast members visits the city somewhere in the plotline.

Or, again in Manchester, there was a commercial

shot with professional footballer Robin van Persie advertising a famous training shoes manufacturer, during which he is seen kicking a football about with his son under a very scary (for me) steel-beamed railway bridge.

And, there's more... an episode in series 8 or 9 of the now-discontinued 'New Tricks' BBC television programme had the backdrop of a road-crossing railway bridge running through the storyline. I had to stop watching the TV screen when cast members were standing right next to the monstrosity whilst delivering their lines, instead preferring to listen to the dialogue until I knew it was 'safe' for me to start watching again.

Silly old me? If you think so then you do not understand phobias, nor what they can do to phobics.

A couple of other TV commercials that have shown these nasties in the course of the ads include two irritating moustachioed idiots for an over-hyped telephone operating service, while carring what looks like a blow-up doll version of a train.

And, TV presenter James Corden is seen driving through a series of green lights and under several railway bridges in a commercial for a well-known insurance comparison website...

Is This Phobia Limited
To Just Me?

I can't be so naive as to think that I am the only person to be suffering from this particular phobia.

Or am I?

I can't even find a descriptive 'obia' name anywhere for the irrational approach I have towards railway bridges, so that in itself says to me that my phobia is pretty much unique.

Here's another 'for instance' observation about what I am trying to get at. I dislike (hate would be a better word) mushrooms with a passion. For many years I thought that I was the only person in the world who cannot stand them. Then, all of a sudden, I came into contact with several other like-minded mushroom-haters, through work, new friendships and so on. I was no longer alone with my adverse feelings towards fungi as an edible foodstuff.

I thought I'd found an appropriate 'obia' to describe my railway bridge phobia, but it wasn't to be. *Gephyrophobia* (pronounced jeff-eye-ro-phobia) is a fear of bridges but, on further investigation, I found that it meant a fear of crossing bridges. That is totally not what my problem is all about unless, of course, somebody suspends a rope bridge across the Cheddar Gorge in Somerset and then suggests I walk across it at sword point.

However, one description I found for gephyrophobia comes very near to how I feel when I am within viewing distance of a railway bridge across the road. The description states: *"You get light-headed, dizzy; your heart races. You become afraid that you'll feel trapped."* In other words, a classic, old-fashioned panic attack, and that pretty much sums up not only my own feelings at the point of 'impact' but ,also, the feelings of every other phobia sufferer on this planet when they come face to face with their worst nightmare scenario.

There are those that have an irrational fear about spiders *(arachnophobia)*, constipation *(coprosta-sophobia)*, clouds *(nephophobia)*, trees *(dendro-phobia)*, flying *(aerophobia)*, going outdoors *(agorophobia)*, enclosed spaces *(claustrophobia)*, childbirth *(tocophobia)*, heights *(acrophobia and/or hypsophobia)*, nudity *(gymnophobia)*, peanut butter sticking in your mouth *(arachibuty-rophobia)*, thunder and lightning *(brontophobia)*, mirrors *(catoptrophobia)*, clowns *(coulrophobia)*, and so on.

As you can see, they and many, many more all have names for their fears. So, why does the bad karma I feel towards the sight of railway bridges not have the honour of an 'obia' status? That's surely discriminatory against the few of us (or just me) who have got this unwanted, unasked for and unexplainable hang-up.

Or perhaps my not standing the sight of railway bridges comes under the generic 'obia' for everything, which is *panaphobia* and/or *pantophobia*?

Two other 'obias' that came quite close, but no cigar, are *siderodromophobia* (the fear of trains, railways or train travel) and *siderophobia* (the fear of steel). I don't have a direct problem with trains, railway lines or even train travel, as I used to catch the 08:18 train from Petts Wood to London Bridge every weekday morning, and the 17:36 back again every evening for several years, back in the 1970s, with no fear except, maybe, that I would have to stand all the way to Grove Park on the way home! And I do not have a general fear of steel. So those two 'obias' can also be ruled out.

And, for the record, the fear of peanut butter sticking in your mouth *(arachibutyrophobia)*, mentioned on page 52, doesn't really exist. It was a made-up 'obia' for a Peanuts cartoon strip story from many years ago, and it appears to have a cult following for continued usage. However, some people in this world believe it to be a true phobia, which says a lot about their perception and attitude towards phobias.

Considering the fact that I can't find an 'obia' to describe my own phobia, and I have yet to meet someone who genuinely suffers with the same problem regarding railway bridges, I have to consider myself as being unique.

What the London & Greenwich railway viaduct looked like back in 1837

The Reaction of Friends, Family & Strangers

To be fair, not many of my closest allies, let alone passing acquaintances, knew of my phobia. But, of the ones that did already know, I have always had mixed reactions from them.

I have already written briefly about a trip I made to Boulogne in France with some friends way back in 1988. I really had a panic when I saw the large railway bridge across the road ahead of us. Fortunately for me, those friends did not laugh at my predicament. They were kind enough to appreciate the fact that I've got this strange phobia, and also to curtail their walk to accompany me back to the relative safety of Boulogne town centre.

I'd probably ruined a potentially good exploratory stroll for them. But, was I being selfish by wanting to turn back? Hmmm. Most probably, but unintentionally so, yet desperate times call for desperate measures and my phobia was demanding that I turned back. The fact that my companions also returned with me was their own decision, which was probably more influenced by my outward appearance and demeanour than anything I may have said to request them to do an about-turn.

I do not think that any of my immediate family members ever understood my predicament. Then again, I am not sure how many of my siblings know that I suffer from this affliction. Myra thinks it is barmy that railway bridges spook me; I was showing her the photo of the Ludgate Hill railway bridge from 1927 (this can be seen on page 44) one day and she asked what was scary about it.

That just about sums up the reaction I get from most of those who learn of my phobia and don't understand it. Just because *they* don't have a problem with railway bridges, they can't seem to be able to find any reason why *I* should have a hang-up about them.

So a restless and embarrassing time is experienced by me trying to explain what I shouldn't really need to explain - that it's a *phobia*, that's what phobias *do* to sufferers and... *I didn't ask for it!*

Is There A Solution?

Or, more succinctly, do I wish to be 'cured'?

This is where a phobia becomes a very controversial topic. There are experts who claim that 'cognitive behavioural therapy' is an ideal solution.

But is it?

Or is it something that can be achieved through a sufferer's own mindset by their inbuilt willpower?

And at far less expense than paying someone to 'instruct' phobics to make them face their fear head on?

Alas, all the willpower in the world isn't going to get me to walk where I fear to tread or look. Besides, I'm too long in the tooth now to worry myself about looking for a 'cure'. I needed such remedial work when I was a nipper, not in upper middle age.

Let's look a bit more into 'cognitive behavioural therapy' anyway. The crux of the matter is to physically face up to the fear and then, by a process of 'one step closer' situations (usually involving paying someone a hefty fee for the privilege of this advice), you become more and more 'appreciative' and 'happy' within the previously hostile environment. That's apparently referred to as 'exposure therapy'. I hear it works great for those people with phobias about spiders, rats, snakes and such like. But, for great big steel railway bridges...?

I *know* that I have a morbid and inexplicable fear of railway bridges; I've had it nearly all my life, after all. I consider myself to be strong-willed when the situation or occasion calls for it, but if I can't control this problem then how in the world is forcing me to visit sites that have always given me such anxiety going to 'cure' me?

Broken down into bitesize nibbles, 'exposure therapy' is supposed to work in the following order. My feelings on the format are included after each sub-heading, in italics:

Reveal the mystery behind the phobia trigger.
Yeah, right, what mysteries do railway bridges hold... apart from the illogical reason for scaring the crap out of me?

Think all the time about the thing that frightens.
Er, no thanks, it's bad enough spending much of my time trying <u>not</u> to think about them!

Seek out pictures and photos of the nemesis

and study them.
Whaaat?! Railway bridges scare me witless as it is, so why would I want to sit and study images of the bloody things? I don't think <u>that's</u> going to happen in my lifetime; it was bad enough when I had to study and choose the photos to be included in this book.

Continue to look at the photos until they no longer seem to be scary.
Hmmm. That will take a long, long time for me, I am sure. And, even then, if it <u>did</u> work I am cynical enough to understand that what you look at in a picture isn't quite like facing the real thing... not by a country mile.

Confront the problem head-on.
Aaagh! In other words, for me, that means going and standing under or directly facing the one thing that makes me entirely uncomfortable. That has got <u>zero</u> chance of happening in my case; as I've said before, this type of approach may work for (much) smaller items like rodents, arachnids and reptiles, but I have grave reservations that confronting or standing under a railway bridge will absolve me of all phobic tendencies I feel towards it and its steel-laden accomplices.

I would like to think that someone, somewhere knows of a cure for my phobia, without it necessitating the hard-to-believe ritual of a "get a bit closer, now closer still" approach.

Please don't get me wrong here.. These are purely my own reactive views and I am sure that many other people with phobias get a lot of satisfaction from this approach. It's just that I cannot see myself being one of them.

When I searched on the internet recently, for copyright-free photographs in the public domain of railway bridges (and, in particular, the 'viaduct' in the Spa Road vicinity of Bermondsey) to include in this book, I was suddenly confronted with a screen full of them. Apart from immediately breaking out into a cold sweat, I found I just couldn't look at them, despite the fact they were *only photos on a website*. I had to cover most of my field of vision with one hand whilst using the computer mouse with my other hand to click away from that site. *That* is how badly I suffer with my phobia... and *that* is why I do not believe that 'exposure therapy' (especially the parts relating to studying pictures and photos of my nemesis) will work for me.

When Jerry Dowlen emailed me the photos he'd taken of some railway bridges, my central nervous system created havoc each time I clicked on one of his attachment links. I had to force myself to view the photos and then appropriately crop them for inclusion in this book. *I hated every moment of it.*

It's not a darkness thing, either. Yes, it can be very black underneath long arches and bridges, yet from a young age (maybe even younger than when I first clapped eyes on the Bermondsey viaduct) I have not been able to sleep well if too much light is trying to burst through the closed bedroom curtains. Even when I used to work night shifts, I would block out the daylight by attaching unrolled black dustbin liners along the length of the wire that holds the net curtains up!

Maybe someday in the future, some professor will hit upon the 'phobia gene' and successfully find a way to eradicate it. Right now, that's science fiction to me, but as we all know from past experience, science fiction has an uncanny way of becoming science fact, as man's understanding of this world and everything that's encompassed within it improves and becomes more knowledgeable.

I have found that writing this book has helped me to get the problem off my chest; it has allowed me to call out, "I have this phobia. I am NOT a freak!!" But I am still unable to shake off the stigma of going anywhere near railway bridges and, at my age, I have to accept that I must continue dodging them like the plague until I leave this mortal coil. The fear, irrational or otherwise, has accompanied me on my life's journey and I suppose, to reiterate what I said on page 54, I must think along the lines that this strange phenomenon has made me a unique individual.

RAILWAY BRIDGE FACT

Every railway bridge has to be individually measured and designed to fit its intended surroundings. It's not a case of 'one size fits all' where these eyesores are concerned.

Folkestone Central Railway Bridge
Photo: ©2016 Trevor Mulligan

As I enter my twilight years, I can look back and pat myself on the back for succeeding for the most part in avoiding my phobia being force fed beyond manageability. It's a bit late in the day, I'm a bit long in the tooth, too much dust has settled, and any other clichés that fit here, for me to go chasing around all the railway bridges in this country to see if the 'exposure therapy' would work; that's what it would mean doing, because no two railway bridges are the same, unlike all the spiders with their eight legs who creep around menacingly, all rats that just look sinister or all snakes that slither along on their legless bodies.

Conclusion

One of the strangest, even ironic, things about my phobia towards railway bridges is that the town where I now live has several steel-structured bridges spanning the roads. The place has even got a huge viaduct which spans the deep Foord valley, as well as a tunnel road and walkway burrowed under one of the elevated areas, which spans Guildhall Street North.

Most of the bridges I try to avoid if I am walking, and the viaduct doesn't bother me, as it is just a larger version of the one in St Mary Cray that I grew up with. With 19 arches, the Foord viaduct boasts ten more than its Cray Valley counterpart.

Folkestone Viaduct across Foord Road. Photo: Copyright ©2016 Trevor Mulligan

What I prefer to relate to as *proper* viaducts do not tend to worry me. I guess that's because I grew up in a village where one existed before I came along.

The old sketch picture on page 27, which shows what the viaduct in Bermondsey once looked like before its widened expansions and additions, gives a reflection of what a viaduct is supposed to look like in my own opinion. The strange set-up of the wooden stairway on the outside of the arches, which led up to the platforms from ground level, looks quite imaginative but the picture itself indicates just how much extra space was available in Bermondsey in the mid-1800s before all the expansion took place.

And things are destined to get even more congested there, as Thameslink are involved in constructing a new rail service alongside the existing expanded viaduct. Called the Bermondsey 'dive-under', I understand that the new line will descend to road level at Bermondsey and cut through an existing road bridge or tunnel before ascending again as it heads towards London Bridge. No doubt the planners have thought long and hard over that new addition, but just how the system will work in practice, and how it will impact on the residential, business and road attributes in the immediate area remains to be seen.

Another good example of a railway viaduct can be viewed spanning the Darenth Valley in Kent. There's several more examples scattered about the British Isles countryside, although I've never personally visited many of them. A good example of a railway viaduct can be found in Tenby, South Wales, which we delighted in seeing when we holidayed there back in the 1990s.

 The famous ornate Holborn Viaduct in Central London would indicate that it is also a rail bridge, but in fact it carries the main A40 road which links London to Fishguard in Wales. Beneath Holborn Viaduct runs Farringdon Street. I have visited this district of London several times when I worked in the City, and I have never had any qualms about walking under this bridge.

Although I have never visited the area to see it for myself, the Ribblehead Viaduct in North Yorkshire is meant to be one of the best examples of that type of railway support. I've seen photos of that viaduct and it seems to stretch for miles; perhaps it does, as too does the Bermondsey to Greenwich viaduct, but then the Ribble Valley appears to remain unspoilt by a metropolitan expansion that has, in my eyes, uglified what was a serene location in South-East London.

So, why did I decide to write about my phobia, if it is so painful to face up to? Well, firstly, I was rather hoping that it would help me to try and better understand my morbid fear and, secondly, that the subject matter of phobias may just encourage other people to write about their own irrational behaviour when confronted with their own particular personal nemeses. Phobias should be out in the open, not so that the idiots of this world can ridicule sufferers, but so that those same ignoramuses and even normal-minded people can learn to understand what phobics have to push themselves through, twenty-four hours a day, three-hundred-and-sixty-five days a year (plus one extra day in leap years!).

I hope that this book has gone at least part of the way along the road to achieving that and, if only one person reads this book and acts by writing about their own phobia, my goal will have been reached.

THE END

About The Author

Much of the time you will see the 'About The Author' pages in books written in the third person tense. You know the sort of thing... "*he* has had acclaimed success with *his* debut novel..." and so on.  Indeed, I've been guilty of it myself when including my bio in previously printed work.

So now I am going to break with tradition and tell it to you from my own mouth, as though you were seated here in this room with me.

I was born in Farnborough Hospital, between Orpington and Bromley, in the mid-1950s. Yes, that does make me a 'baby boomer' product, and also 'rather old' at the time of preparing this book. But, hey, I've lived a colourful, although not always favourable, life along the way.

Most of my childhood, teens and pre-marital years involved growing up in St Mary Cray and Orpington, and part of the time in Dulwich, south-east London.

My parents originated from South-East London long before the Greater London boundary extended into North-West Kent. My paternal grandparents were South Londoners, while my maternal grandparents' roots are in Suffolk before they moved to South London. Mum and Dad moved out to Orpington and St Mary Cray not long before I was born; Mum worked for both the TMC and Morphy Richards electronics factories along Cray Avenue, whilst my Dad ran up and down the stairs as a conductor on the number 51 double-decker bus, collecting the fares between Orpington and Woolwich.

I now live in 'retirement' on the Kent coast at Folkestone, but most of my time is taken up caring for my dear wife, Myra, whose disabling illness worsens with each passing day. It's a full time job that 'doesn't pay well', but the alternatives don't bear thinking about.

Anyway, nice to have met you, and I hope that you have enjoyed this book.

Trevor Mulligan

For the record, I have absolutely nothing against the people or the area of Bermondsey whatsoever, apart from the sprawling viaduct which I speak about in this book. I cannot help the phobic intolerance that I have towards an inanimate object other people treat as 'the norm'.

OTHER BOOK TITLES
BY THIS AUTHOR

Rediscovering... The ORPINGTON Car

The true story behind this now long-forgotten but once iconic little car. Designed by company director Frank Smith, the Orpington was produced by Smith & Milroy Ltd, at their factory workshop in Orpington in the 1920s.

Copies of this book have been selling well locally at The Croft Tea Room, St Mary Cray, and at the Orpington Library. It is also available from Amazon, both as a printed book and Kindle-ready ebook.

Amazon (Printed Paperback)
ASIN: 0957312903

Amazon (Kindle eBook)
ASIN: B00COCS8LK

Kaleidoscope Patterns
Colouring Books

All 6 Volumes Available Online From Amazon
(Printed Paperback)

VOLUME 1 ASIN: 1517395275
VOLUME 2 ASIN: 1517421128
VOLUME 3 ASIN: 1517426227
VOLUME 4 ASIN: 1517426405
VOLUME 5 ASIN: 1517454670
VOLUME 6 ASIN: 1517529719

Kindle-Ready
Interactive Quiz eBooks

Five Titles Currently Available
From Amazon

GENERAL KNOW. ASIN: B00C3W2YA2
WORLD HISTORY ASIN: B00C41Q45S
MOVIE FAVOURITES ASIN: B00C3TK150
ASSOC. FOOTBALL ASIN: B00C3SFB60
WORLD SPORTS ASIN: B00C3TVVSG

Poetry Genius
Or Poetic Mayhem?
Poems like you've never read before.
Probably.

This book contains a small collection of verse written by the author during several changing periods of his life. Some may say the work is simple, others may say that it is cute. Some (but probably not everyone) may even say that it is outstanding... or even astounding. It is, however, for each individual person to read and understand the poems, either selectively or collectively, based on what is printed on the pages in front of them.

Poetry Genius Or Poetic Mayhem? does not follow the style of any poet in particular, or any other poet at all, as the reader will quickly come to realise.

Available now on Amazon.

ASIN: 1537555081